O F

B E I N G

N E I G H B O R S

OF BEING NEIGHBORS

POEMS BY

DANIEL BIEGELSON

Dear Jeff -

Thank you for your support
and for hosting this
amazing reading series.

Yours in poetry -

Daniel Ross Biegelson
3/18/23

dbiegels@hotmail.com

Copyright © 2021 by Daniel Biegelson
All rights reserved

Cover Art by Margot de Korte

Cover Design and Interior Layout by David Wojciechowski / www.davidwojo.com

Published by Ricochet Editions / www.ricocheteditions.com

Ricochet titles are distributed by Small Press Distribution
This title is also available for purchase directly from the publisher
www.spdbooks.org / 800-869-7553

Library of Congress Cataloging-in-Publication Data
of being neighbors / Daniel Biegelson
Library of Congress Control Number 2021933499
Biegelson, Daniel
ISBN 9781938900396
9 8 7 6 5 4 3 2 1
FIRST EDITION

FOR AMY, JACK AND JUNE

CONTENTS

"…mind's claim to independence announces its claim to domination"

—Theodor W. Adorno

"There is a ladder
The ladder is always there."

—Adrienne Rich

"the footprints inside us
iterate the footprints outside"

—C.D. Wright

NEIGHBORS (I)

"History has made us all neighbors"
—Rabbi Abraham Joshua Heschel

Replace I with you. Replace clouds with branches. Exculpate my heart. Replace my heart with another organ. The eyes. With iris aperture. Or. Hear the body with the body. Extinguish the inner ear. Imagine the scrollwork. There are times when assent is impossible. Hear the way the syllables sound. The words ring. Excise the plague of grasshoppers from the crisp fields, the schoolyards, the white lawns. Recall the patch of pin oak leaves against a backdrop of memorial sky. Fingernail the edges and pull. Walk in rubber soles. Refuse leather. Unless to bind the arms. To wrap the forehead in tefillin. You are made in whose image. Replace neighbor with children. Redact silence since silence is impossible. Also a cymbal. See. A symbol. Replace symbol with synapse. Move on to arrive at the synagogue. Because I believe I am angered by the slightest hiss. Imagine a parade drumming around the town square. The brick-and-mortar courthouse with a hint of roman tracery. See the angles. From various angles. Above. Treeward. Though the legs. The limbs. The thrown pink and blue bubblegum scattering under lawn chairs. Scrambling. Redact stained glass. As a child entering to see swastikas spray-painted on the ark. Now again. Plagued. And plagued by continuity. Layer upon layer. Bewildering specificity subsumed by synchronicity. A ritual. We chronicle. Replace message with memory with message. We feel the past lifted upon us. Differently then. Now again. I am rage but plagued by a hibernating guilt. A cryogenic wood frog. I told myself. This is a safe place. Saved by people. Which people. I had children. I have children. I am afraid of revelation. I am until the sun shines. Once I tried to set aside you. Try again. Once I tried to set aside rage. I keep finding myself driving down the highway confusing blown tires with black crows. They've have been circling for eternity. Do you believe in eternity. Infinity. Affinity. For once. Can we pray without ropes around the prayer. Exchange branches for wires. Extinguish the clouds. We are the murmuration turning over the earth with our predatory eyes. We are the field turned over and under. We want to preserve our singularity. We can no longer look at each other.

THE LIGHT WALKS OTHER AVENUES

"*I can / connect / any two things / that's g-d*"
—*Eileen Myles*

I would have followed the light everywhere even
            at sparkfall. Instead, I go mourning all day
and flitting about the hollow space inside.
            In the marketplace headless chickens hang
against the closed dark of a butcher's shop.
            Past the gerrymandered edges of town, a farmer
rowing the heated earth in the faint orange afterglow
            finds a fossilized ribcage. Should we be nostalgic.
Utopic. Under the light now the light of eternity.
            The field eighty years on still warmed by magma.
The plates still grinding their bitter teeth. And now
            I have broken with the remnant of you that lived
somewhere among the archives of my many selves.
            A break so sudden that words flood the streets,
the anabatic wind hunts and the trees clutch
            their purses. Do you see it too. The way the details
shake loose of their moorings. The way silence
            cannot suffice. And now it's you breaking
with an image of me. Let me lean down. To assist.
            What do the seeds know. I have a strange
relationship with time. Just yesterday
            an *I* in me stood eating pea soup and crusty bread
with utensils owned by people we had forgotten
            while you waited for your predictions to resolve
or dissolve. Some iteration of the world is always ending.
            Even upon reasoned review. Burning.
Little is up in wings again as the sky is enumerated.
            The salted veins excavated for inspection and prayer.
A form of protest. We see and do not see ourselves
            there. We sway and nod. A drying sea. Is the sermon
enough. Is it inimical. No one says I sent a packet of actions
            to *The New Yorker*. No one submits their liver
to *The Los Angeles Times*. No one crawls toward
            the hovel or speaks the word. No one draws

back the shroud. It's one foot. Then the other. 'Onwrds.'

Pray with your 'legs,' your walking and all I can do is to find the clearing.
Not even the threads of the threadbare story.

And even here in the last rays of empire when it is so easy
to return hate with hate, the obscure light wraps

itself around our heartened bodies and hums.

George Oppen

Frederick Douglass;
Rabbi Abraham Joshua
Heschel

Our eyes come into being over time and we begin
        to solve their intricate limitations by embracing
the dark and invisible spectrums of light.
        And there is darkness, if not silence.
And despite market forces, they are not interchangeable.
        Still life. Still light is the subject and object.

Elie Weisel

'And this must be sufficient.' For you, I would have stomped
        grapes on my march to Rome past painted billboards
of naked women or watched *I Love Lucy* in dubbed Italian
        while dust blew in through the balcony. This is silly
and growing slim or slack—an American condition—
        growing virulent and violent. What is this you ask
as the fires burn and glass breaks. How far can I go before
        we unravel. My first bicycle was a royal blue
Schwinn with metal flecks that sparkled as I road in circles
        under the afternoon sun. And I felt like a Wright brother
or an actor playing a Wright brother on a set
        of a Spaghetti Western. We met in the crinkling rain
or on the bus or by walking backwards with brown-bagged groceries
        through an apartment door and we are told at once
everything that has happened to us could have happened

Bob Hope via Martin
Luther King, Jr.

        in no other way. Could never have happened. And 'if by chance
we develop hiccups on taking off—we will "hic" in Los Angeles
        and "cup" in New York City.' Where I am waiting

John Gallaher

at JFK, attuned to the news, 'watching the national tragedy,'
        the global tragedy, 'this personal tragedy,
we wake to each morning.' I am trying not to love
        with a closed heart. I am split like an atom.
I have many brothers who are sisters
        and sisters who are brothers and many who are many.
This is far afield from where we began.

The part I love best is the part I don't know at all.
        You rattles at irreplaceable hours
without end. *You* argues the slow turn
        from light to dark or dark to light
should be sharpened into a quick blink.
        My eyes. Your eyes. A world
without. The origin of imagination. We stare. It hums. Ask
        Ann/Ask Abby. Is there a gift without a giver. We estranged
down the avenue and other avenues. Buried
        love with an eye to digging it up again. Thought
we sang songs genetic. In our bones. Bore our bodies
        in an open casket. Exhumed them from ditches.
Then the baseball team migrated
        and the empty stadium ripened for demolition.
And all spins 'outward and nothing collapses'
        into nothing. Accidents colliding with anti-accidents.
What is the equation that explains the future. Whatever
        follows answers. Regardless of intent. We walked
backwards into or from a storm lit evening. Deny
        the mortar. Deny even the fire. Hold the wreckage.
A part of me is stone. A part of you is air.
        And now our children leap from the stoop
onto the pavement with dust organs jostling
        and dust hair streaming with dust teeth clinking
and dust words dissolving. Peer out of rows upon rows of tents
        with wind in their lungs and wind rushing past
their ears and wind closing their unopened eyes.

Walt Whitman

7

ARCHEOLOGY OF AIR

Let me know if you've heard this one before—
a squall of starlings in love with the evening cutworm
        occupy a winter field
the stubs of no-till stalks signal
        an advance in the architecture
of living and morning
carries a scent of snow.

I withdraw. So the perennial landscape persists.
Everything is deferred and deferred
again. I can't resist
        the metaphorical apple cart
with its hint of honey and the bare presence
of people. One starling
startles and the field empties.

Or this one—
you have to imagine a window
to look out a window. Looking
out a window of broad sunlight
          you have to find the seam.

You have to find the seam
to envision the harbor
as a blown sheet of darkened glass
or the starlings as passenger pigeons
          in an upright world.

Nothing surprises anymore
in an empire of apologies.

Let me begin again—
you have moved and left me
with no forwarding address.

In the giving I am gone
and what travels homeward
travels toward a begotten space.

We are not mended in the mending.

I am closer to an industrial skyline than I had imagined.
        I am an asphalt lot behind
the chain-linked fence
but before the refinery towers.
I am in love with pretense.
I am a dark field before the foothills
        and a torrent of snow. The snow
and the foothills
now imaginary graces.
The imaginary graces now
murmurations of snow.

Be still. Slight sleight of hand. I am
sorry for the elegies I wrote
        before we died
words left in the white hills
when G-d was simply a bird.

THE NEW LIGHT

"all shall be well, and all shall be well,
and all manner of thing shall be well."
—*Julian of Norwich*

The sign written in a sharpie says *Be Right Back*
and through the window the light is spilling
or flooding or creeping from the backroom
in the café on Green Street where I'm hungry
again. Today, I am obsessed with addition,
not so much form. Listen, why is the angel
of death so easily confused. I was born yesterday
and the day before and the day before. I read
about a study in the *Star-Ledger* with a cup
of coffee, a brie and arugula sandwich
on French bread that put some old habits
in a new light. If I love popcorn, must I love
oblivion. I'm having a child, must I grow serious.
My grandmother's dementia colluded with cataract
to close the door of words. I'm writing about
something resembling wisdom. Why is safety
still a privilege. Who is the we that dreams of husks
of burned out buses. Who is the we drinking lead
laden water. Who is the we that inscribes or enshrines
the dusk. Which we slowly rolls their rusted
dodge pick up behind me for a block as I walk
after services and then screeches past with tires
burning. Bumper stickers clarifying the air
of suspicion. What sort of reader are you. Am I.
I make birdhouses. I digress. I look like my father
and my mother and the waiter from tomorrow
if tomorrow ever darts inward. The apples in
the basket next to the muffins on the glass counter
have the look of something looked at or looked over
or the sheen of something else. *Terrible*. *Terrible* says
the bald owner with a white apron and blue plaid shirt
in the corner as he turns off the endless news. I've been passing.
Fearful. Cycling different *yous* to the surfaces. Once

I was invited over to an apartment where confederate flags
and torn pages of swimsuit models holding AK-47s
and strapped with combat knives hid the walls and no one
seemed to notice that I was made of ash. I stood.
I stand in my body. How can I pass on what I bury.
It is impossible to forget the names of flowers after talking
with the florist next door. You would think the weeds
would be different, but they have names—yarrow,
clover, thistle, buttercup, ragwort—and someone
in every language knows them all. I've succeeded
in distracting myself from myself. Have you come
with me. Where the night flutters. I have waited
too long weighing a bouquet—birds of paradise
against roses and baby's breath. Why not a spray
of Queen Anne's lace. It is snowing again.
And I am afraid I have lived too long inside myself
to be to anyone. It is snowing again. And I am afraid
of the kingdom of ends. You see additions
upon stammering additions. I feel guilty for making
love with you. Listen, this is too personal
to be a confession. Apologies gather wherever socks
go when they go seeking their mates. It's a particular
and universal dilemma like the way our legs knock
and piston as we use our opposable toes to free
our feet. This is silly and serious. My son now.
My daughter now—there is a fire in the house,
in the house of annuals, the house of memory, the house
that houses nations. Are we trapped in the trappings
of metaphor. The house of perennials is already
an umber field and we are not born into a cloud
of knowing or unknowing. It is a problem
of simultaneity—and & and & and. We must be
born with this third thing about us or in us
or elsewhere—a grain of an unheard echo. A seed. No,
that's not quite right. We don't really speak anymore
of what it means to be human. As if we were dying.
We speak of clothes and their cast. Of cars and rigs
mangling people. Of grievance and violence. Shuttering
or drifting toward a mass extinction. Can we convince

ourselves that we are real. Is this need. The passed down
Kiddush cup is a pocket watch is a daguerreotype is a trope
in a poem that says *Be right back* when 'love is what we mean'

William Bronk

14

NEIGHBORS (II)

Replace period with break. Plant windbreakers on the prairie. Lilting grass turned under. Replace eye for an eye. Distinguish the hall of photographs from the cemetery. Pack a basket and blanket. Eloquent green lawn. In the windowless breakroom, the hum of the innards. The 'things of dry hours.' You could be anyone. Inquire after yourself. You are parking. Gentle with the maroon door. Pulled by stubborn sky. Dropping off kids at daycare. Exchange a dollar for four quarters. *Even here you are someone's lover. You take it with you. All love is same love.* Replace love with need. Redact need. Need. Is uneven. The need for gratitude. Is absolute. The bread baked on stone does not have time to rise. We wonder. Yesterday you were a neighbor. Replace neighbor with television. 'Your head becomes a TV hull / a gargoyle mirror.' Your head gleams in the sunlight. A parade of parents rotates through the circle lot. Pollinators round a Rudbeckia's black eye. We call to each other. Exchange parents with children. We arrive today. Made other. A human inhuman process. Processed. We arrive today. We thought we were going home to tomorrow. A progress of peonies. Redact home. Replace my home with your home. We feel the need to pass people on to each other. Birds too and other animals. It makes more sense in language. As abstract. I want to recoil now. Don't know what to call you commonly. We see but do not see the same thing. We hear but do not hear the perpetual murmur of the wind beyond the trees.

Gwendolyn Brooks

Mary Karr

WE LIVE IN AN UNKNOWN SEA

City of secondary egresses or flightless egrets. Everything contains or radiates commentary. The v's above diminished and misplaced. North and south reduced—a redaction of climate. Trees move west. No handholds. No guardrails but passengers suspended in the tiled light of the subway terminal. There is someone there standing with one hand holding a bouquet in a hurry to apologize and stave off an ending or hurried at the proposition of making love or both or anxious to hit the shrinking window of visiting hours at the hospital around the corner or to make a daughter's first grade recital or to reach the Long Island cemeteries before rush hour. The sky we cannot see does not speak. It burns. It gnaws. Tracks rust off into darkness. The bare concrete persists but cracks. The footholds threaten to widen. Water seeps up from below. Lost in a different darkness. Will we slip through. Into. Will the flashing shadows speak to us in another language. When you were younger you stacked stones upon stones. Placed some in your pocket. In easy forgetfulness. Now they are too heavy to take out.

A) WHEN THE CLOUDS BREAK SUGGESTS A SUDDEN UPHEAVAL IN THE HEART

a quick spike in the ratio of light to dark, but really we are not better equipped for a slow dispensation of wind licking away at a cloudbank until cloudless, the sky folds into a particle driven evening. Naturally, the epiphany assumes a point of departure. Say the sky or the body. But the sky is replaceable. For now. It lives in me. An ellipsis of pelicans hovers over the waves. Some words full of rain overcast the sky. But how to leave the body behind. Or which body do we occupy. One of mine is a ship whose husk/hull, rusted open, looks like a baying wolf. Lope through the understory. Wind wave of grass. Loop me in to your compact. Your inscape secret. The delicate epidermis and vellus hair. The hands hiding in pockets. To begin to return. From distance or immersion. From a point of loss and gain. To begin.

B) WHEN THE CLOUDS BREAK TO REVEAL
A CITY OF BRICK OR GLASS

Allen Ginsberg

Wilco

Bob Dylan

steel girder or tinted and tilted skies. Coastline or seawall. Surge. How can the market keep rising without a question mark. Is this too far afield for something so serious. 'I am trying to come to the point'—the antenna sends and receives. 'I am trying to break your heart'— the earth tides and the sea tides rise and subside. Incrementally or suddenly. We work and we compose—'the conductor he's weary / he's still stuck on the line.' And will be some day beyond us as the arc shuttles us along. Glaciers fall to the ocean and take on a different identity. Why must we bear witness to believe. To return to the impossible point of departure. The train takes us to a city once a forest and a forest once a city. We pass demolished buildings and rusted I-beams and rebar spokes and cars stacked upon cars. We hope and alter little. We return to the terrestrial. The dark territory. The night terrors. The night sky stirs in retreat from the earth—a turbid string of starlight.

C) WHEN THE CLOUDS BREAK WE TAKE IN
A KIND OF DAILY REPETITION

or feel a similitude to the sermon upon our skin. 'Don't fight it, feel it.' Why. Imagine the Sam Cooke
white cumulous clouds above pasted to a weatherman's blue screen. Then banter, a bad joke
about hair spray, dogs jumping into kiddie pools and a segment on housing starts. Am I a
commercial break in sea of the same. A haven. What do I advertise. Is my body replaceable
to you. Can we turn out and over. Begin again out of loam rich with flood plain risk and root
upwards like the snowdrop. The tiny star of violet petals hoisted aloft. The downtown loft
gutted. You see. A gutted epistemology: there is no sea. Currently. I wanted to be a parcel of
air. 'You send me.' Where. How do we sign our own demise. How do we leave and persist. Sam Cooke
You can't break something and then break it again. You are the syntax of my own otherness.
May I be so to you. At least briefly. A gift. For what do we really know 'as the earth begins Patricia Goedicke
to end' again. Call out. My deep beautiful splinter. Wrap me in the arms of the visible and
invisible alike.

NEIGHBORS (III)

"…because in times like these
to have you listen at all, it's necessary
to talk about trees."
—*Adrienne Rich*

Replace glass heart with scalpel. Words become a cudgel. Call for rain. Glisten. Close up. Magnify a leaf until the drop brims with color. Replace leaf with wind. Every June we lose limbs to straight-line winds—elm, maple, oak, ash, etc., etc. They come knocking at night. Redact redundancy. Extinguish the list. Insert space. Remove the catalog. Remove, stack, and mulch the dead wood. Map my internal geography. I am a bowl of cold plums. Would you have one. I am a body of words in uproar and otherwise. Replace words with birds. Fill a tree. Take your pick. Redact free will. Replace map with mine. Relieve the workers. Every day we leave labor(s) behind. Exchange our labor(s) with neighbor(s). The dark soil laced with slender roots swells and subsides beneath us. As the tide. Breathing. Who are you. Extinguish the implicit. We are 'an answer' which leads to another answer. Some of us are no longer breathing. I am used to defending the singularity of our experiences, but grow concerned about reducing the dead to their individuality. Redact redeem. We linger longer in blue light. We are not only what we say or do.

Rabbi Abraham Joshua
Heschel

20

WE MOVE IN ABUNDANCE

It's a ridiculous argument, but my son stands his ground. Why can't he attach a balloon to a teacup and fly to New Jersey. Why is our neighbor's yard filled with dandelions and drift. Why do you own a house and not a home. Why do you mow the lawn and despise clover. It's bedtime. The fawn is speckled. Tears the grass up. So the roots dangle. From the mouth. Does the gardenia sleep in a garden bed. Go to sleep. With stars. My G-d. Go to sleep.

And what about the column of air above. The water rights below. Why is the ground so hard even after rain. Why do I keep falling in love with words when words mean less. Petrichor. Petrichor. Bless my children. בָּרוּךְ. בָּרוּךְ. בָּרוּךְ What have years done to this poem. Catastrophe upon catastrophe. Each to each. As layers of sediment disparately touch. Why is a bell ringing. Why do we long for a past we never lived or even visited like tourists in Neil Young t-shirts staring into an Icelandic volcano. Why does my friend solder stained glass windows in his garage at night. Fumbling with light. Why a bell ringing. Why do I assume all the hives of my life exist somewhere still as if I could walk into any one again and end somehow here. Why do I feel guilty. For writing this poem. The privilege. What marks us. Helps us. Makes us legible. Think other of us.

Someone is playing a violin on the subway platform again. Someone has an open case of cast coins and a few fisted dollars. Someone has a litter of roses. Someone is holding hands with someone. Someone in white kicks tips upright on their toes to see the light pouring out from the tunnel. Someone's headphones look like earmuffs. Someone is playing with a bow, gracefully easing along strings, when the shooting begins again and people we know and don't know scream and crouch, scatter and dive, cover heads and fall.

Do we experience the same violence. From the inside out. The outside in. Save it and store it and feed it to each other. Wildly or gently as poison. At the same table. Over passing conversation. At the same altar. Over passing prayer. Bitter. Brittle. Stone. My G-d. Who is not mine. Or ours. Here. Some of us go on to bend down and tie our laces as torrents of people pour past. Some of us go on to lift up faces from the blue light of our phones and shift stream. Go on to clamber out of dreams. Climb stairs and clatter into the evening air. Float off like balloons. Uniformly distinct. Rendered and unredeemable. Earthly and inhuman.

THE METAPHORICAL HEART

My son stops putting together
a puzzle of the solar system to pronounce
   I'm really stumped today.
Then asks *What does stumped mean.* Confused.
Stymied. *What does confused mean.*
For weeks, I couldn't read or watch TV
   after the photograph
the unbreathing
boy on the beach
face down in the shallow surf
arms to his side and knees
tucked slightly under
the way a three-year-old who still
toddles in stilted balancing steps sleeps
   bright red t-shirt and sneakers
hair neatly combed by the water.
And above and wrapped in gray gauze. *The sky*
   yawned. The sky is quite
hungry. The sky eats the clouds for dinner
my daughter riffs in extended soliloquy
   as she leaps from a couch
to the hassock scrambling to reach me.
My son says *My heart was made to wave*
   as I head out the door to work.
My daughter replies *My heart is made of apples*
   as I bend to kiss her head.

Maybe the metaphorical heart
   is supposed to ease the wound
of disagreement with the open flesh
of the world. Maybe its design
is to lift us to repair.
Maybe we are born singed
and signed. Though now maybe
is a galvanized steel pail
hauled to the pasture

with its bottom rusted out
and the heart
magma incinerating
its way through the chest.
Eyes burning too. The horses thirsting
behind the barbed wire.
And this fails. And fails again.

And 'I am sick of the spirt' of capital.   Gerald Stern
'Whole families shopping at night!   Allen Ginsberg
Aisles full of husbands! Wives
in the avocados, babies in the tomatoes.'
The logic of distraction. The logic of the uncanny
        at the center of a centerless
universe—that philosophical
understanding of distance. Of desire.
Of death. Of drowning.

Can I begin again. Without order.
Without reference. Without image or idol.
Can I carry you a while.
        Is my uselessness useful. I know
I know that I can't
speak for you. And really. 'All I ever wanted   Edward Hopper
        was to paint sunlight
                on the side of a barn.'

But I see what I see. Differently.
In the afterbirth.
Of afterbirth.
A breeze stirs his hair.
Inanimate words vibrate
        clap as lit leaves pinwheel.
The elm again.
The trick, I think,
        is to have each foot planted
in a disparate present.

Each standing in deep
and distant laceration.

Dear reader. Inside and out.
Are we afraid. I know what I want to say.
        But not sure I have permission.
As my son puts another piece
of the sun together.

Purple clematis wraps around the black mailbox.
Leaf stems curl around the thin netting. Are you

held by the tendril of sky just outside the frame.
Heirloom marigolds bought from Mennonites

at a farmer's market bloom from shaken seed
year after year. After all this, somehow we arrived

at couplets. 'The arc of the moral universe is long,
but it bends.' 'A curve is but a straight line frightened

Martin Luther King, Jr.

Edmond Jabès

by its own daring.' In my meta-heart I know I would
marry you again. Though for all our place settings,

there is an empty seat. Forgive me for what I want
to say. When every close breath smells of milk

and feels like a betrayal of every vibrating atom.
You see me. The uprooted trees alter the earth. Forever

and ever. And lastly the land will hold us both
even as we cling to ourselves and break open into flower.

Unethical to transfigure the refugee boy
        into a migratory bird
and more so solitary

does all translation promise a return
is all translation a signatory to the original
'which will one day find
        the bull's eye of your hearts'
for better or worse

Now I am struggling to reverse the sea
        of leaves raining
the bitter wind hunts and the desperate
roots walk

Pablo Neruda

Once I tried to set aside rage. I kept
finding myself driving down the highway
rushing toward storms of my own volition
where even the long grasses and swales
of trees would go wild in projected protest.
Until the earth grows cold and clouds
rearrange the sky. And in the distance
the tail of a pickup rears out of a ditch
its red lights gleaming in a sudden late
April freeze. I can hear the ping of ice
on the windshield, feel the slight fishtail
and then the car ghosting into a spin.

Once I tried to set aside rage. I kept
tying and retying your small shoes.
Once I held onto rage—for better
or worse—let it drive me to the other
side of whatever dark veil
descends and divides us
holds us back from where the carrier
pigeon returns and graft saves
the orange and you keep dissolving
and becoming another you.

You see a red shirt. I see a bird.
I was thinking of other words
to complicate the sentence.
Then I was thinking of other images
to corroborate my feelings. The storm
cracked branch twined still
to the braided elm (again)
hangs on to its dime leaves
which mimic the wind
and will hold their serrated shade
of green for a few more months.
Then I was thinking of other people
I paid to love for me in so many ways
when I was out of ways to love. Then
I changed one letter and arrived in a place
just further/farther down the road.
Though it seems this is about me
it is really about you. I said no more
sparrows as if they were as rain and cloud.
I apologized for confusing purple finches
with house wrens. I collected old lumber
parcel numbers and obituaries.
Waiting for repair. I felt my basket
of allotted sky empty. Then I thought
I should stop burying the lead. Incomplete
apologies gather in the streets to protest.
I am examining the repercussions
of ownership again. Imagine
the multiverse at your door.
Imagine adding to the circumference
of the puzzled sun. Say
nothing or. You are still waiting
to be hailed on a busy boulevard
by a stranger who calls your name

and fills your cup—which is also her cup

       which is also his cup

which is also their cup—past the brim.

Dear you.
You again. You exceed yourself and me. You misremember
        a white bee in clover. You make a necklace.
Any you could wear. Gather mock strawberries. Where.

T.S. Eliot

We know they grow. This is how we speak 'each to each.'
        Past each other. Calling loudly.

Dear me.
Even in the smallest disclosure there is specificity
        and such specificity burns. Remind me again.
It burns with alacrity
burns in comparison by incredulity.

Dear you.
In some far off sense
            in the way clouds are conjunctions
or the way words tend to cluster
            just as they form or pile up
unused at the end of pages
a sparrow is not a bird but a category.

Dear me.
The paradox of how not to love and how to love
            language   as fire
resides in comparison.
What do I do with all of my nuclear reactions.
How many kinds of light can we name.

Dear you.
You can burn a house to cinder
          or heat a home.
Be thankful. Be sorry. Bee sting.
I admire the vexing begonias
in the coconut fibers hanging
under the eaves of the porch darkening
through the day and the couplets stumbling
home from their disked fields and gray offices
puddled construction sites and warehouses
tropical restaurants and corrugated factories
jigsaw lots and halogen lit classrooms
alluding to other words in the dwindling light.

Dear me.
The temperature drops and grass turns blue.
Sound and cluster. Couple together. Tighter. You
are on the outer rim. Send a bee shiver. Remember
          to cycle to the warm heart. In and out.
I am equal parts you & you & you.

A.P.
Hill
Now I'm thinking
simultaneously of reportage
and wind sprints. The red wool
shirt rides upon a roan horse.
I am as surprised as you
to meet him here. At this point
in the century. The already
always politics of death camps
masquerading as love
of khakis and self. Certainly
certainty is the enemy.
Do you see. Do you
prefer a faith full
of questions. Standing here.
Standing there. Somewhere
someone weaves a flag
from the pages of a book
and sets it on fire. Maybe
I mean metonymy.
Finding common root.
My cup runs over.
The gravity of it all
pulls at us.

In the meta-universe a skyscraper
       rises in a small town in the Midwest.
A black hole grows in a 'cosmic boondocks.'
       Let me learn my bitter heart.
Even when I say *all is quiet*
       I ask a question.
Even when I try to speak clearly
       directly I veer into vectors.
This is how I know you love me.
       Dear G-d. I refuse.
We replaced the porch light—a bronze
       facsimile of a kerosene lantern.
Open the door into the guarded night.
       Will you be present even if by proxy
when every child enters the covenant.

And speaking of which, I wore
my Met's cap into Royal's country
yesterday. Yesterday exhausted
its relationship to today. Dear
G-d. I've been given
fits and false starts. I'm having
trouble separating out
the innocuous. My heart
is small. I am not
ashamed or freed.
What did you say
about distraction.
But this poem
could go on
forever and ever.

How does disease enter the world. I have loved
        you always like the abrupt
toad that interrupts the night's quiet.

Hear now. We are closer.
Time is a language of lulls and whispers
        suddenly of remarkable terror.

I realize that *suddenly* is another way
of saying *look* for no good epiphany.
All my bedtimes stories go *and then*
and then…

Why are all ghosts
blind. Like
shifting stories. Maybe
I mean personification.
The book has eyes.

Go to sleep. With stars. You cannot see.

We may linger as the remainder
        of a contradiction. We cannot stop
the sentence from starting over.   The constellations
        of connotations depend   at times upon
the continent. Did you see your face
in the face of your father.   Your mother.   The sky
        threatens to burst
open with the squalor of cicadas
        or a chorus of rain. We circle about
a subject—you
        misremember a turkey buzzard
feasting beside a late blooming dogwood
        and then you remember the misremembrance.
Then a sparrow hawk too. Try again. 'Try to ignore   Richard Hugo
        the hymn coming from the white frame' synagogue.
You can hear it as you walk past with your shepherd.
There is the boy on a beach. Another. And another.
        'Like every sparrow falling, like every grain of sand.'
In every iteration. And inside   Bob Dylan
my son adds another puzzle piece to the sun.

Some things are not yours. Not today. Not tomorrow.
Put that back. We are called. It goes on.

Each word we utter follows another word
into the universe. Impossible to distinguish

one from the other in a stanza of echoes
the sensual formation

of which we may be made or entangled.
A soft mouth may feed you

persuade you to ripen and open
—gloss skin of red honey crisp cut

white petals flecked with black—a hole
in space around which the white bee hums.

Once on either side you said you saw
two moons in a dark variant of sky.

We are dead and we are not dead
and all our lives

of numbered evenings
suture into one.

NEIGHBORS (IV)

Replace dog with brother. Take walks on burnt grass and return under treeless sky. Exchange directives for best practices. Practice your run along the fence line. Monarchs and swallowtails carry on along the highways lined with a cosmos of causal wildflowers. Extinguish your artificial sense of silence. You let your dog shit in my yard. Where my children run barefoot circling each other around the white pine. The ocean levels rise. Mortgage rates rise. Don't pretend to love one another. Turn your predatory beak. Redact the brackish ocean. Turn it black and red. Exchange ocean for consumption. Predatory lending of labor. Be still. We are the colony of bees in collapse and also the tractor trailer stocked with hives and the long-haul driver on the CB radio and the farmers waiting for pollinators. See the red dust clouds rolling. See the black clouds closing. A tongue over top lip. Bite hard and rain. Extinguish the dog barking. Redact the self. Exchange dog for children. Barking for howling. There is a wall 'dressed / with bits of broken bottles' beyond which our labor persists without us and we don't dare to look. Replace words with words. Yours or mine. We don't act upon what we see. Redact the sea. We are the murmuration leafing out over the highway. Pouring over the sky. We suffer decentered as we imagine stone. Human again. We don't know each other at all.

Eugenio Montale

WE CARRY OURSELVES EVERYWHERE

even to places we have not been and will not go. A flutter of pigeons feast on a loaf of bread outside the corner bakery and end up on someone's twitter feed. The window's daily consolation of blue sky strengthens and diminishes. A chorus of roses in white five-gallon buckets. Swatches of fruit fill a stand on the west side of the street. Sentences suddenly dead end in observation. In the constative. On their way to what was once a Woolworth's the rear door of the truck shutters open. Parakeets in boxes and feathers poking through air holes. A flurry of moths at the glass. Next year we must remember to misremember. No, that's not quite right. To keep our secrets we must lapse into a portrait of stillness or wrap them like future gifts. We discover them again as a wind of need bearing a squall of obligation. We open the door and sing ourselves inside. A few blocks over forgotten gaslights persist. It is not raining across the way.

I HAVE TO GO NOW, I DON'T WANT TO GO

Are we oriented. Feeling winter pelt our eyelids. A rattle of cloud at first until the snow shakes loose and wind tears off the peaks of waves. Scatters the breakers into white streamers. Turn around and around.

Are we joined. Are we lead back to what we know. Eating falafel or opening a window to let the dry heat of the radiator escape or walking hand in hand to the bedroom. Let us tend to tenderness. This time with the moonlight masquerading as a skin of frost.

Invert a world. Turn the room inside out. I'm watching Otis live at Monterey again ecstatically ripping up *I've Been Loving You Too Long* and trying not to imagine his body after the plane crash. It's strange to fly. To be so self-indulgent. To pack my concealed self. Tucked under the seat with a heavy coat. With children kneeling, standing, crisscrossing again and again in the seat. Peering out at the earth and the things built out of the earth. The same. To project a whole sense of wonder.

For a long time I dreamt of an unknowing sleep. At night I still keep a whisper watch to hear you breathing. Stand in the frame obedient against the darkness. Do you keep a 'diamond in your mind.' A sound that takes shape. Edged forests below drift into cloud.

Tom Waits and Kathleen Brennan via Solomon Burke

We're building airplanes with digital screens for windows. I'm trying very hard not to get lost in the loss of a single person. I am hurtling toward disappointment. I am not amused. Entertained. I have distance to keep me close.

In the snow and ice the flightless bird waits to sing at the sight of a single greenish-white egg. Define redemption. I can pronounce the words without any idea as to what they mean and so I hear the uncanny everywhere. And I pray to pray. Shake the truth from the tree.

'I don't want to stop now.' 'I don't want to sit down.' It is embarrassing to live between so many intimacies and so sometimes I forget to call out to my other selves. We are here. They echo. And perhaps we sing simply to sing or simply to give ourselves away.

Otis Redding; O.V. Wright

I GAVE MY LOVE A CHERRY THAT HAD NO STONE

for Ruth Suzanne Levitz

The marble façade appears pear in pollen light. Then orange. The peach ripens. Imagine a time-lapse. Terracotta pot on the sill above the radiator where the paned glass clouds. White specks of vermiculite against the deep soil. The planted seed from which the green leaves unfurl a pause. A compression. Maybe a persimmons. And beyond a coastguard cutter cuts whitewash. I am a camera with a bug's eye. Reverse course. Take a course in oils. Acrylics. See the wings struggling to close in the common wind. Hair like scrolls of parchment paper. Find an abode in the present. A butterfly exhibit. Fold each of us into each other. Who promises us telos. The night sky sifts down darkening a small dot of trees. The evening dusk lacks precision. Go down. Come down. From the tinfoil loft. Onto the sidewalk to discover the green tempered shards of the busted-out GM station wagon window. Brother. Sister. We were too young and too loved to be frightened. Now the wharf more creosote than wood gestures across the river. Now dark clouds darken with red smoke. An expanse of fear spreads before us. A forest. We live at a distance. Temporal and temporary. And sometimes we suture. The endings together. I knew. I should have flown to your funeral. Or your unveiling. I should have placed the stone still imprisoned in my pocket. I'm having trouble with revision. I never knew your other name. I'm second-guessing my predilections. But you gave me permission. This is public and private. The family a property. 'The Holy One smote the angel of death, Chad Gadya who slew the slaughterer, who killed the ox, that drank the water that extinguished the fire that burned the stick.' I stand where others stand. Truer as we move. What did the mirror hold for you. A child encloses every flash of light and flick of dark in each room she touches. What do you enfold. Intend. Keep your hands off. You say. Stay out of the street. Outside a game of hopscotch erased by rain. A game of double-dutch on hold. You had been running behind yourself this whole way. Now the tealight burns the paper boat set upon the water. A brown hint of smoke stretches until invisible. Now we wait our turn. Who plays you in the second act. Who do we serve. When do we eat the persimmons. I wash my hands and pull the Sam Cooke blossoms right off the lower branches. 'How can there be a cherry that has no stone.' Collage together vowels. Let loose from the given image. Maybe we part with each other by stepping into another self. Is this the lesson from a distance. Maybe you gave me permission. And now the sky persists in its bearing—opal or pearl, rose quartz or turquoise. And this time I have traveled through the whole day without touching its darker permeations. Holding still in preparation.

NEIGHBORS (V)

Replace subject with object. Object with subject. I am having trouble remembering. Part of the problem of resisting. Is. Instant. Gratification. System degradation. 'Whoever degrades Walt Whitman another degrades me.' Some people want to be objects. I suppose but briefly. But what form. Formlessness. The commodity. Redact the parking lot. See the thornless honey locusts. Left unscathed by the emerald ash borer. Replace borer with Asian carp. Pause. Backspace. An act of text and imprint upon words strung together unevenly across time. Replace time with town. See the July bunting against the red brick storefronts. Chart your responses. Insert parenthesis. You know them by their coin leaves. There are no more dime stores. See the isles of aisles of emptiness. Smile. You have a dimple. Smile you are on a bodycam. Who do you serve. Someone other than you. I want to believe some forms can be extinguished. From a distance. Nothing changes. Everything can burn. Can be ash. Review the question mark. I'm curling my hippocampus toes around your toes. 'My mind is made up. There is Allen Ginsberg going to be trouble.' Let's unpack the first part first. 'One day it occurred to the Members Aesop of the Body that they were doing all the work and the Belly was having all the food.' One day it occurred to you that the body politic makes some of us a feasting plague. I am. A card-carrying member. Here is the black gleaming ladder of obstruction. I mean abstraction. The bush along the riverbed exhales lilac. Not flames but flames. Ready for rapture you suffer. A deviated septum. September kept us warmer longer, but the little scent was gone and when I came up for air you reminded me to replace the faucet lines in the apartment next door. *I've had this wrench for a long time* my alter ego said *but sometimes it forgets that it wants to be a wrench.* The grandmother in teal sweatpants nodded. Said *yes.* She had coffee cake. I wanted to be a neighbor. Replace neighbor with plumber. Why either/or. What do you contain/release. The problem. Exchange problem with plums. Savor when offered. So sweet. We are not so intimate as lace seems to indicate. What is want. I want a plumb line and depthlessness. You see the way we have sold you. Called you. Human capital. When 'all you have is a hammer.' Abraham Maslow 'If I had a hammer.' Build a stage. Replace stage with self. Do the murmurations above the Pete Seeger bone white sycamores perchance perform. Does it seem a seamless scene. Replace scene with surgery. You had me in stiches. I love your curved nose. Now I linger. Redact I. Who am I talking to and where are you a person burning. 'I am trying to come to the point.' Where. Tell Allen Ginsberg me. Hear. Hurry. Hurry. Here.

BUT FOR THE GRACE

Up and down the wrought iron alley fire escape people come
and go. Even the uninvited come and go. Even the dog
someone sometimes uses for a napkin when no one is looking.
The dog is in love. So am I. Here is where you might expect
to hear the Big O's *Try A Little Tenderness*. People pass through
the galley kitchen and no one has seen Nancy since the incident
with the ginger-spiced muffins. I notice a pattern
and fill in the futures. On the Orchard Street rooftops
whole families stared backwards into the night.
I know because I've read it somewhere or seen it in a movie
or because it was my family too and had I been born
I would be dead. This isn't the place I imagined.
I am broken which is different though similar to being
empty. It turns out Americans are making less
love, which make sense since even in the imaginary
privacy of our own bedrooms we hate what we've become.
There is a kind of truth that's true whether or not you believe
and a kind of truth that's true because you repeat it
and one lives without you and the other needs permission.
In the suburbs the black crows are next, then goldfinches
and hummingbirds last because they are small and solitary.
Speak up. If this sounds familiar and you despise the Vermeer
and the gold lacquer, we are getting somewhere closer to tomorrow.
Inside the apartment, the dog pads over. I wasn't aware at first
but it was my voice that called the dog. We all occupy a place
occupied. Sometimes I hear children kicking a ball to each other
across the dirt and into turned over garbage cans. Sometimes
all I can I hear is the scratching of rocks. I hear the bird
call of a screen door opening and closing into the alleyway.
Strictly speaking, this is a kind of prayer. The animals
that have entered our orbit are mulling mutiny. 'All
the rabbits saying' no. 'All the frogs saying' no.
The animals who are a part of our living and dying.
The mumbling rattle threatens like a sodden sky. Does joy
lead us to extend joy. Here is the cup and here
is the waiting chair. When we sing do we increase the song

Muriel Rukeyser

44

of the world. Have we prepared the table. We stand
on the curb waiting for a car to arrive late on a humid night
in a city of heights looking over to the other side
of the street: the row is halogen lit, most windows
barred, a few stoops and a frame without an awning.
We can hear the rise and fall of people joined to people.
Are we coming or going. Even the uninvited are punctual.

THE ABSURDITY OF CARRYING AN UMBRELLA WHEN
ALL YOU NEED IS OILED FEATHERS

Yesterday on a mission at the Natural Museum of History we found the Peekskill meteor displayed in ochre lights beside a photograph of the red chevy malibu it hit. Who is the we in that sentence. My son. My daughter. Maybe. Who else is here to imagine a field held in shadow. The crackling of a sparkler throwing off radiant embers. A grainy video of the pulse interrupting a Pennsylvania football game. A dog barking as the sky snaps with light. A grammar of following faces.

Is this absurd. Are you unable to hear. Do you constantly speak. Are you obedient. Why do we assume the future with the same conditioned obsession as bargain hunters in tortoise shell glasses clicking kitchen utensils into coded shopping carts. Who is the we in that sentence. Extend an invitation. Why a ringing. We seldom listen. Why turnstiles and revolving cages. You have a better chance of being snatched up in a tornado and then hit by lightning and swallowed by a hurricane.

Inside a life-sized replica of a blue whale hangs from the ceiling. You can hear the piped in ocean bending, moaning, whimpering, whistling. I could go on & on. What is your name/names. Would it be different if you were handing out miniature bibles with green vinyl covers. The rain descends in sheets. Then stops. Do you know the trees speak to each other. Their roots reach out to each other. Send sugar through to the suffering. Even under the pavement. Even the small frayed filaments.

A light appears and disappears in the tunnel below. You have seen its slow braze before. Now you are not a witness. This time the heat hits your face through the grates. Turns your eyes off. And yet. And yet. Sounds like a sonnet. You are stung. So gently. White bee upon bee. Look at how we have time-traveled and shifted through space. A part of the performance. Who is the we in that sentence. What do we accomplish eating a salted pretzel at the hot dog stand. Waiting for falafel. Scent of grilled onion in the air. Circling the wreathed lions and the police officers in kevlar vests as the sunlight slants and your children play with children they have never met who speak languages they do not speak.

Who is the we. Who is you. Who are we constantly talking to. I too am conversing with the air. You are not the only person present. Subway doors gasp open. Passengers spill out. If we take communion to the limit, will we come back mute. Why a ringing. Will we have time to turn all our faces. Do the dead die in us. Are we the dead wood set to be limbed. Do you hear a siren or the crackle of a walkie-talkie. What have we dropped that alters the earth.

What artifact stolen from the hall of error. The metaphorical heart murmurs. You can see the monastic pieces leap into expression. You can still hear a hiss from the origin of a universe. A static swelling. Going. Going. You 'want to see everything clearly, even through the fog.' Claude Monet The smoke. Gone. So how. How do we learn to carry each other without carrying each other. Through every yesterday and every tomorrow. History is the history of hands. And yet we resist. We resist our own totality. And yet we turn. We must. Turn our eyes back on.

EVERY MEETING IS A HALLUCINATION WAITING TO HAPPEN

Then I was back in it.
The War was on. Outside
—Elizabeth Bishop

and tomorrow when I wake up will be tomorrow
and I will know because I will remember
eating river ruby grapefruit for breakfast and ignoring
the raisin bran, giving thanks for the bodily openings
that I know are not optional, calling my sister
at the EPA office with the struggling fichus or from
the office with institutional art that warrants a slow zoom
to frame the drop of sunlight on the mermaid carved
into the prow of the clipper ship to talk about paintings
that are not paintings or the discovery of a tumor
or a new black hole or a universe without dark matter,
calling my brother to check in about his test results
and to ask how my nephew in remote classes
is getting on in school, sleepily driving past the conoco
that hours before was an exxon and lingering over
the business model, breaking warm bread over
French press coffee in a studio apartment in the shadows
of bitterroot mountains, glaring pines shrink-wrapped
in snow or saguaro cacti with a panoply of white eyes,
or aspens blinking like silver coins cast into sky,
delivering a baby roadside into a world that did
and did not exist moments ago. It happens. Maybe
I imagine myself a doula or an EMT on the way home
from the bar after a long night and a longer shift
or a cattle rancher with a bit of practice in delivering
calves who glimpsed the car run out of gas on the shoulder.
At which point, I have to wonder. A great many things.
Like when does it all stop. Is it a decision in us.
Or like how do I become vested or move on past
my injuries. Or like 'who is the you before whom I
am I.' The truth is that to get through most moments
I imagine myself on the other side of the earth. One
half of me cloud. The other a subset of nomadic facts.

Rabbi Avraham Yehoshua
Heshel

48

One half waiting for the other half to catch up. And
I am constantly casting the one part forward
like a sidewinder, hopefully with enough force so
that the rest of me is lifted along or at least dragged
down the way as tin cans tied to the bumper of a cadillac
or like a cartoon character who has somehow managed
to tie his own ankle to an acme anvil. Maybe I am
the weight on the world of others. Maybe the cloud
of dust kicked up by the sudden exit or awaited entrance.
Maybe I am the fading line on the highway or the machine
marking the line or the orange and white traffic cones
or the clown fish in the pediatric aquarium whose job
is to occupy the sick and the contained. And here it ends,
as abruptly, arbitrarily or involuntarily, as it always does
where it always ends—'in the middle of the road

Carlos Drummond de
Andrade translated by
Elizabeth Bishop

is a stone.' Minha amiga, 'there is a stone in the middle
of the road.' And now a pebble in my shoe as a terrible
reminder. Pick. Pick it out. I put it in my mouth, just under
the tongue. Run now. Try to follow yourself. 'Falling. Falling.'

Elizabeth Bishop

Try. I'll try to expel myself or explain my inability to assimilate
or make choices in hopes of avoiding closure. Keep. I'll keep
my vessel close. Thoughts closer. 'And now we see through

1 Corinthians 13:12

a glass, darkly; but soon face to face' as in the skit where you
play someone else looking through an empty frame at yourself
and later you watch as you make a public appearance on
daytime television. And what is it that time makes
possible—the you that was then and the you that is now
and the you that may or may not exist sit in a waiting room
of needful silence. And what else goes unrecognized beside
the interrupting call from behind the door. The gorilla who
strolls into the middle of the basketball court, faces
the camera and thumps his chest and then departs. What else.
When the cries become crying. When the war is in here too.

NEIGHBORS (VI)

*"O fragment of mica, looking on which I once learned, for the
first time, that I is not something 'in me'"*
—*Martin Buber*

Replace male with electrical socket. Female with power plant. Rip through the drywall. Wind the cord. I wish I was an umbilical. Too easy. Too domestic. Too binary. Insert a question. We are bonded. Not strangled. Experience entanglement. Redact. Post bail. We used bailing wire to hold together the pallet compost bins. Purple sweet potato vines leaf out in spades. Dangle through the slats and begin to creep across the lawn. You said shadows tiptoe too. Hear the tinkering. Replace sense with sound. Hear the wind in the folds of the flag. Move the catcalling/caterwauling crowd. Students chant in t-shirts/without t-shirts. Students

Bob Dylan chant slurs. A spectacle of intimidation. 'They're selling postcards of.' But these are children. Smiling. Are these children. The diagnosis predicts. A dicey. A disturbing. A runaway. Recovery. Replace diagnosis with daisies. Daises with fortuneteller. Are you surefooted. Find me. Redact me. Since I is failing. I is fleeting. I is missing. I is a place. And another. We enter. Thick flies swarm melon rinds. The green sugar pumpkins return to half-ripen. An ocean of grass opens before my daughter as she totters. Redact the sea. The people sway/are swayed.

George Oppen Which people. Are you. Redact the human view. 'The ledges in the rough sea seen from the road / the harbor.' We are safe. Are we safe. We blasted bedrock. Laid bare before. Made roads from here to there and from there to here. Where is here. Replace where with when. Replace safe with saved. Replace saved with salve. I am approaching you with eager tenderness. Try a little. I've seen you. Arm pulling your casted daughter close. Parroting hate. Replace hate with love. Is it real. Real to me. Replace me with you. I am writing my own extinction. I am fixated on becoming a port. Plug in. Replace he with she. She with he. They with they. Come closer. Down here. See the turtle bug. Lovely parted shield of basil green. Whose work dissolves. Our work. Your work. Replace a cloud of birds with a squall of starlings. See the hidden reptiles beak the earth. Refuse/refute prehistory. It is in us always. Redact always. See the grain in the granite. The flakes of mica. Replace the present with the ever present presence of universal possession. West to east and east to west. We are the gathering of seafoam on the descending outcrop. We are the leaves drenched in sunlight and samaras spinning through the air. Today clarity. This is the sky. This is the crosswalk. I wanted to say the children. The bright children are bright. Are laughing. Are not frightened. Are still children. But you are not prepared to be you.

HENNY PENNY BLUES

For while in Borough Park everyone's grandfather died
        of a heart attack on the subway
though we found this generational and subject
        to an apoplectic shift in wind.
How did *Little* cross an ocean. Speaking Spanish.   Chicken Little
        Yiddish in steel holds. Most of us don't know
what it means to be native and too many of us go on
        pretending. Not much has changed.
The firmament is falling. Fading. Failing.
        Words too. 'Early North Jersey industrial skyline'   Bruce Springsteen
frozen and extraterrestrial, 'a lunar landscape'
        Composed by senses. And sentences.
And song. Then 'it took dominion everywhere.'   Wallace Stevens
        So. We love and love what is not ours
and ours to love. So. I pull my raw hands
        into the sleeves of my coat
weave through the sidewalk's torrent and attend
        to the surface of things. The surface trembles.
So. I am burying the thought that leads
        to another thought. It's endless.
Impossible now to dig up. We cannot
        be quiet even in our most intimate whisper.
Even when we find ourselves without our other selves.
        So. I am charging myself with a misdemeanor.
Lately, I've started to encounter dead birds
        in the most unexpected places. Hallway closets,
dustbins, behind the cans of kidney beans in the supermarket,
        inside pink cowboy boots, lying on stools
in elevators, in the boxes of finely watermarked paper
        our grandfathers labored over—the numbers
grow. I imagine too the dead birds in tiny fedoras
        and wool suits. What other gestures
 of class might our earthly grandfathers have wrapped
        around themselves to court our grandmothers.
We've been thrown back onto the shards
        of questions we thought we had answered.

It is absurd what we do to each other.
          And one day *Little* names a successor
and the sky is suspended until further notice.
          Pull the tarp over the glistening green field.
Listen to broadcasters banter. Fade into nightly
          irrelevance. When *Little* returns he finds
smaller particulates. When *Little* returns

Lightnin' Hopkins   he finds himself 'loose in the sundown.' I am loosed
upon the wind. The gold watch with engraving
          upon the gears hidden from sight
passes from one pocket to another.
          And maybe, someday, past the evening eclipse,

Matthew Arnold past forgiveness, we'll walk 'where the sea meets
          the moon-blanched land' and sit as the waves
wash up the Rockaway sand and envelope us.
          We'll see a beach cleared of connotations—
bright and ready to be returned.

IT'S DIFFICULT TO STOP THINKING ABOUT A CADILLAC ORBITING THE EARTH

Take my hand.   First my mind in your hand.   What are   you now?
—*Muriel Rukeyser*

Today I'm reading an article about health care in a newspaper that isn't a newspaper if we take the process of pulping trees immediately and forgo 'the inter-related structure of reality.' You are trying to write about your mother with Alzheimer's without being flippant and I'm trying not to write about you. 'Everybody's serious but me.' You don't say. It's almost folksy or whimsical as a replanted cutting. You sitting with a stalk of dallisgrass dangling from your lips on the tailgate of a pickup or leapfrogging the curb through the arch of water from an open fire hydrant. What does the light illuminate. Sometimes we forget how strange it is to be uncommonly commonly embodied. Sometimes I wake up from a dream and sometimes I dream until I wake up. Sometimes I repeat myself to pinch myself. Sometimes I see a moon sliced in squares on the plaster chalk white walls and forget I'm here. Beside you. Forget you. The walls inside this poem come from a rent-controlled apartment near Steinway Street in Queens. Sometimes I get confused. There is another place I go and you come here. Where is here. The page is electrical ether.

So, I replied when I oversaw a photograph of your mother who has since passed. *Everything looks like something else from a distance or up close* and then felt instantly guilty. Guilt's cousin, embarrassment, lurks somewhere in the attic upstairs on TV where it's all asbestos and floral drapes and a flicker above using the metal cap of the chimney as a sound system. It's the sixties again and I'm being glib. I'm time traveling along the depthless surface like a green basilisk bicycling its back legs. You see. You know I know Barry Gibbs through Jimmy Fallon and someday you won't know Jimmy at all. I prefer Colbert. I hate disco and kitsch. Who am I kidding. Behind all my pauses. The lit world comes in upside down. I remember her grey eyes ringed by a white film and the way she no longer seemed to blink from the other side of the laminate table. Bright orange peaches drowning in syrup and a white plastic spork. They make them in a rainbow of colors. It's not as obvious as you think. O—I almost used a semicolon. Someone told me that they were as sinister as a newly minted/blasted strip mall/mine. I remember her swaying. A sparkler casting a child's smile upon her face. Her 'teeth were bad.' She hated her dentures. Look over your shoulder. Pull the drawer open and sink a pencil into a rotten honey crisp. When I was little I used to eat McIntosh, but now can't find them in grocery stores or orchards. Sometimes I think about moving to Canada.

At the Scotchwood Diner, my grandmother's food was always cold, and I was always tipping apologies to the waitstaff. There is something cartoonish and horrific about things falling

Martin Luther King, Jr.

Allen Ginsberg

Li Po

George Oppen

into a category. What saves us from assumption. Consumption. The fire. What saves us from

Martin Luther King, Jr.

ourselves. *We should never forget that everything Adolf Hitler did in Germany was "legal" and everything the Hungarian freedom fighters did in Hungary was "illegal."* What is our recourse. Our course to resist. Part of me comes from a village in Austria that no longer exists. Part of me comes from a port in Puerto Rico that barely persists. Satellites glide across the night sky and some day at some hour one burns or crashes. Space stations too. Once returning home from the city, I found my goldfish drifting, frozen in a white fungus. If you are a passenger pigeon like me, you know what I mean. It's cold in space. You were worried the other day about turning people into art. No. It's more like turning art into art. One of the many things we already are, so I suppose it's a matter of theft or abstraction, pulping or fracking as opposed to objectification. I object. Which happens almost always. In sitcoms. Or maybe it's more first order instead of second. Either way, we're ready to press our fingers to the glass. In other words. I find myself speaking to myself.

National Geographic

And it turns out we're mostly a 'menagerie of microbes.' Or electrical storms. I can't remember. Hold the door open. Steady. Swing both legs at once. Place both of your hands with linen-thin skin on my shoulders. I pulled you softly up from the elbows. I held you leaning. The seat soaking. Do you see what's missing. The generosity of absence. Are you on the outside pulled inside by the address to gentleness. Through and through I could feel your bones. I've always wanted to be the sand through which water weaves. Dear you. You are somebody else now. A part of the method. On your way. What happens next.

NEIGHBORS (VII)

Replace O with only one. See Spot. See Spot run. Replace Dick with Jane. Neither says the Testament. You have. Selective reading syndrome. Does disorder matter. Is there. Chaos. Balance. Recall the molecular models from your Ms./Mr. Mueller's chemistry class. They are they. Are you inside. Exchange inside for outside. The frame. Now implicated by address. Where do you live. Remember. The pink and blue beads of sodium and chloride. Crystal ionic lattice. 'The unsettling sense of missing time.' Memory implies revision. Like the way I worked to forget my two days of braying silence after you told me you were pregnant and only recall returning with a toy turtle. Named after my father. Named after his uncle. Add owl to turtle. Remember for future adaptations. Revise you. You will be someone else later. Redact silence since silence is impossible. Partial. I am mulish. Are you bullish. I look back despite the warning label. Objects appear. Looming. And we felt sporadically guilty when just two our son sang *she can take the dark out of the nighttime / And paint the daytime black* while the elderly couple standing in line at the grocery store behind us were appalled at the miniature apocalypse. Replace partial with pillar. Replace pillar with shadow. Whose head. Sing. Sings 'while you slave.' Where do the headwaters of life begin and end. Revision implies form. 'Do I use all of my fears.' I am not afraid of dying now. Kicked 'loose of the earth.' I am afraid of the earth. For him without him. Be still breathing. The red cedars less than locusts populate the hillsides. Alter an altered place. We have scraped, left bare and unknowingly invited the species. Into fire. The brambles burn. I understand sacrifice. Or some sacrifices. Are you in here with me. Eurydice. Revise. Replace with eschatology. My son now lying on the oak floorboards with his socks pedaling the air. Fitting together wooden train tracks. Soft pine. Male to female. Female to male. We are moved by the rails of language to sight and infection. Cut back on capital. The ivy roots form to fit the surface they climb. Excrete glue then dry. We reinvent the words. Sometimes with simple intonation. Revise the performance. The cadence. Make the words murmur. Make them personal. Rustle as invisible leaves. Return them to the commons. Maybe. Son. My son. And you will ask, *where are the adults*. Replace adults with atoms. 'Here I am.' You are. Look. Here is a ram. And here a door. Here a window. And let me tell you now so later. Little one. I refused. And once. I held. You. Against the metaphorical and G-dly darkness.

Matti Friedman

Bob Dylan

Bob Dylan; Muriel Rukeyser; Joseph Conrad

George Oppen

Genesis 22:1

THE SEA AS FAR AS WE KNOW

Laura Vaccaro Seeger

'Once upon a time an egg and a chicken and a tadpole
and a frog and a seed and a flower and a caterpillar
and a chrysalis and a butterfly' appeared as referents
or walked or swam or sprang or crawled or flitted
in to the *Brass Cat* on Cottage Street in a surreal set-up
with no real send-up. In a sense. And in smaller and larger
terms, cell by cell, the cells made cells. Antecedents
or prisons as numerous as the stars. The words of our
children reinscribe. The punchline before the punchline
steps on the punchline. And we can be sure in the way
we can be sure of things we delimit that we came—

George Oppen

'not from anything we did'—but from our mothers
and their mothers before them and so on and they
came from the sea as far as we know which is why
sometimes we long for weightlessness and are held
in water for months by our mothers because they
are mothers and this is how we know our children
are Jewish and that this is a matrilineal joke you don't
get to tell or if you do it's because I'm already burning.
As a tree. Resin melted. Seeds released into the ash.
No Baltic amber for a generation. The absurdity is in
the repetition. But still. Be still. I believe embodied.
You bring your own laughter as if to the pealing sea.
The boiled egg before you isn't spring, but the white
circle that comes round to death. Quiet now as if
the door is opened into the violent air. Will you permit
me to cry with you, so I too can let go. Of hate. Let go.

the Midrash

Tell me. We are torn. 'The teeth of a locust are the teeth
of a lion' are the teeth of carbon. The pattern maker.
Maybe you are free because you are free to remember
or because you remember as if you were a mother. I can't
remember which is true. You speak every day of your life.
As if we crossed a Rubicon or the Western Interior
Seaway. Seaside. Bankside. We moved to Liberty where
I am a stranger amongst strangers and my neighbor's
children on both sides ask for my church as if insisting

everyone must be a card-carrying member. I belong
to every atom and 'every atom belonging to me as good
belongs to you.' Hear now. Speak 'when you sit at home
and when you walk the way, when you lie down and when
you rise up.' Or close the cloud to rain. The house
finches rosy red nested on top of the claystone column
warm their eggs as if accustomed to the rocking, the coming
and going. I am bound and frightened of the sign. I am
thankful for what we are. What we have received. The sky
is as brilliant as you as a doorpost. We hang our hinges.
The sky folds. Yesterday was as green as my heart as if
my heart was plural, multiple, a multitude, the trees
thinking to the trees as if our thoughts were the same
thoughts as if some of us were inside the architecture
of the song and all of us were humming with our ruby
throats to get in when suddenly my three-year-old
daughter in a hurry to speak before she fell asleep
in the backseat of the maroon car as the sun set said
in a voice as common and uncommon as air, *G-d*
wanted me to be a person, but I wanted to be a bird.

Walt Whitman

Deuteronomy 6:7

HOW MUCH DO I REALLY WANT TO SEE

Once I took a bite of an apple while driving on
cruise control and found a seed inside sprouting
a brilliant green leaf set to unfurl. Immediately
a destination had arrived. Once I bought
two silver goldfish from a Woolworth's and a blue
parakeet though not on the same visit. For the sake
of propriety. Once I brought a snapping turtle hooked
from a pond to elementary school and how it escaped
is a closely guarded secret. Go back. Reverse course.
One part of you is already inside the archives. You
are having trouble with extradition. Wearing a brown
apron, the clerk nets two comet goldfish and drops them
into a plastic bag filled with water and ties the ends
together. Obviously. We jostle through space. Everything
has its analogue. We can't see the hidden punctuation
that differentiates each shadow. We always entered
through the back of the store onto cracked linoleum.
We cut from the parking lot to the front to do shopping
on East Broad Street. I am not manufacturing this though
in a way I am. The means. Of production. As you go.
Onwrds. Hare Krishna. Once I won a goldfish by tossing
a ball into a paper cup where it swam in rings at Saint
Bart's Italian Festival. Later I lost twenty dollars I had
found pounding a mallet to catapult rubber frogs onto
circling metal lily pads. Do I feel guilty. Clear the decks.
The darkness. It's raining. You said it. Not me.
This is regional. I suppose. I am speaking in second-person
again. I am standing in saltwater and exceed myself.
Sometimes variants ripple and disseminate. Simmer. Gesture.
And. Feint. The rain repeatedly sputtering and I think
you would like us to believe in old movies where we stop
before the inevitable sacrifice to call our children
while leaning against the glass of the extinct payphone
to say *sayonara*, where the funerals are fog-filled
and there is always a grave for someone with no one
dug in the orange earth, an uninterested onlooker

with a horse face in a herringbone cap and a shovel over
a shoulder and maybe a shot of dirt falling toward a blue lens,
a thud and a little green world reversed in a rain drop.

NEIGHBORS (VIII)

"The Carriage held but just Ourselves"
—Emily Dickinson

Replace father with mother and mother with father. Stir the dirt with your foot while watching your children jostle against each other at the top of the slide. Shift your weight to lay your head. Lean. Watch the kicked up dust visit us. Replace them with us. Watch us become us. Fun includes, but is not limited to things that happen—cooking while listening to "Bee Tee's Minor Plea," reading a philosophical history of time travel, planting milkweed seeds along the fence line for monarchs, etc.—when you are not lobotomized from fatigue. It is hard to democratize in language. 'A sentence should contain no unnecessary words, a paragraph no unnecessary sentences, for the same reason that a drawing should have no unnecessary lines and a machine no unnecessary parts.' Am I necessary. By whose criteria. Do you believe in revision. Redact revision. You make tiny compromises with the compelling birds. Hear an echo on the thin line. Just overhead. Out of reach. Out of harm. Redact compromises. Be patient. Model patience. Plant also deep pink impatiens and scarlet coleus in the corrugated ceramic pot where they do best. In shade. Mostly. Some sun. Dirt. Always the earth. The purpose to produce production. The model fails. Even in deep beauty. 'A poem is a small (or large) machine made of words. When I say there's nothing sentimental about a poem I mean that there can be no part, as in any other machine, that is redundant.' Am I redundant. I am buoyed by perspective. Rising and falling. Ever so slightly. Imperceptibly. We hover at the edge of resemblance. Where the metaphor fails. We are a minyan of starlings. Exchange starlings for crows. Are you with me. 'Are you being sinister or is this some kind of practical joke.' It is not that I want to deny my culpability. Deny your culpability. But merely to say that we are doing this to ourselves. Do I report the news. Each drive the murmurations grow smaller. It's five am now and I turn over my boot in the dark to hear a child's toy train knock upon the floor. Open. 'In a sense the next thing always belongs.' In the world. There is no other. Only the stranger. Waiting just beyond the sharp edge of the light.

William Strunk

William Carlos Williams

Allen Ginsberg

Richard Hugo

ONLY THE BORROWED LIGHT

Tahara

Tell me what you have seen. What I may not see.
      The space in which every absence is compressed to happen.
I tend to tend to tenderness. Then a mole mistaken for dried blood.
I expect fingernails cut to square a moon.
Behind the double doors, we imagine all ghosts are blind.
We imagine anything can happen.

For the body that lives in two houses there are multiple deaths.
      Every time I remember I know I remember less. Then I embellish.
Dear obsolescence. You inure us. Dear distance. You save us.

People should be treated with a kind of focused attenuation
      'and this must be sufficient.' Light the yahrzeit.
Fill the commandments until the commandments burst.

Some words contain their own light. Phosphorescence.
      Adhesion. Immersion. I hear
with the words and speak with the tongue you have given.

Embrocate an empire of ants, an empire of ends, an empire of root suckering.
      Did I see your face in the face of the deceased.
Even the photographs refuse resemblance.

Forgive the ruthless flame. In mind I can never see the scene. I am being
      abstract. Finding my footing in depthlessness. Lifting
      the sheet of speech as necessary.
Lifting the sheet to clean the thin bicep not your bicep. Lifting
      the sheet to clean the hairless forearm not your forearm.

Elie Wiesel

61

I wanted to hear the lilies. We 'will not survive the earth
        be summoned out of it again.' I wanted to hear the lilies
talking. Out there without wind or water. Out of stillness. I go
with you now. So simply. We bury recovery. Outside
        the lights come on in the enclaves.
A diligent light filling the windows.

May I be for you. May I be more
        like an unseen mockingbird. Be oblique.
More and more myself. Is this translation
        a variation of love. The Queen Anne's lace—descendent
of the carrot—has returned along the roadsides and hills.
Its sudden coronation like a wedding.

Yahrzeit

The low-lidded sky darkens the street until the clouds blow on.
The light silvers and is shaped and I can't recall the movies I've seen
        the books I've read, the prayers I've chanted, the conversations
that would explain my loss or the smallness of the world

or the cross-bracing of the skyscrapers or the life within and I begin
        to stutter—*it was like a swallow, like a flicker.*
I wish for hollow bones, not lightness exactly but density.

Every time I remember I know I remember less. Excise the imagery.
        A bee simply hovers in space. Then embellish. Wings blurred.
Still an emptiness in the frame. A diligent light filled

        the window but whether the light was culled from the room
or drawn from the world we language. You cannot speak. We know we know
less when we know more. What rhymes with disobedience. I am trying
        to distance myself from myself.

The children on their way home, hurry, hoist books overhead.
        Flutter like a line of colored flags in a nautical wind.
The crossing guard waves semantically to the growing line of cars.

You imagined the cars as sharks. You are only your imaginings.

       Now. Are you following. Stop at each address. Hold my hand

as we cross the street. The Queen Anne's lace returns. White bees in translucent bloom.

A light dusting of pollen upon the mandibles though some bees drink tears.

       Now the next in line or order sits in the upright chair left empty yearly.

In forgetting the fireflies transform but today I am in love with birds.

Someone please fill the pitcher. Someone please take the heart to task.

       Beyond any navel. Beyond any song.

All the borrowed light will come to you and teach you how to grieve.

LET THERE BE DARK (OR THE FIFTH CHILD AT THE SEDER FINDS HIMSELF ABANDONED AT A NEW JERSEY CONVENIENCE STORE)

"I love you more than the flame
That limits the world
To the circle it illumines
And excludes all the rest"
—*Rainer Maria Rilke*

On Memorial Day we honor those who have fallen
   into black holes and black holes are a lot like sink holes
my three-year-old son says. You see for some things you need
pauses. Sometimes they function like punchlines. Stop
   hitting me. 'I know what I'm doing.' I am trying
on my body again. The slice of earth we inhabit
   rotates away from the sun. Around the table
with Haggadot open, what does the wise child ask. Everything
   that I am owes something to someone else.
Look up. Beyond the idea of the penultimate moon
   the blackness cast in theory as loose threads
resists some forms of apprehension. Now the lines lie.
Now the geography of time. Now the satellites
   cluster like ideologies of worship
or a miscellany of toys or objects turned to toys.
Now you hear the ring of a pulley on a taut rope
   beating against a steel flag pole.
Do you see the dock and the daysailers. See how we
   arrived at the sea. Now smell the deep creosote
and shiv of salt. Now hear the wind made metronome
   and clock. Now see. Now hear.
The lip of the slurring ocean. Or
   are you the child who does not know
how to ask. To calibrate the past with the present
requires the material senses. Once
   during a training exercise I shared
a chocolate chip cookie with a firefighter
while brush smoldered and could feel
   the practical fire reclaimed by evening sky.

Allen Ginsberg

64

'What is the grass.' 'The moral power.' Now do you see Walt Whitman; Confucius
        the wind in the folds. Speak
your many names. If you know them. No.
        Not yet. May we be inscribed.
Watch my head. My feet. Wash my hands. Water
        from a crystal pitcher. Now do you see
a close up of the palm's creases. What color.
        Now the lattice extends against disorder.
Say I live in exile. Say I live in a room
        inside another room. Look there. We are
liminal and how much do we really know
and how much do we refuse to know. Other universes
        exist. Do you persist. Are you tired
of telos. Somewhere a door opens and invites
on a single digit night a stray dog inside.
       אֵלִיָּהוּ הַנָּבִיא, אֵלִיָּהוּ הַתִּשְׁבִּי, אֵלִיָּהוּ, אֵלִיָּהוּ, אֵלִיָּהוּ הַגִּלְעָדִי.
The door is for you too. Could someone really pay taxes
and feel good about their work. See what is absent.
        See his strong hand. Her strong hand.
See the way every expression contains
        a hint of the figurative. Pull tighter
at navy blue hood strings. Sit on the curb
beneath the green neon QuickChek sign
        next to the township's training yard.
        Is this yours. What is mine.
Blunt your teeth. I want to open up for him. For her.
        A retelling that is an unfamiliar unfolding. A constant
reconfiguration of constellations. It's true
I'm reticent to reveal myself. It's true we overlook
        the natural light of darkness.
It's true we may someday be able to resurrect the patterns
        of ink from the ashes of burned books.
Do you see. Do you hear the expression
        of my genes. Your genes. Now like the rustle
of X through dried cornstalks. A corn snake.
        A copper head. Are you transplanted. A graft.
Graffiti over a mural that becomes another mural.
Are you the fifth child. Where did the others go.
        Are you here too. On the dark plain.

Do you ask or answer. Do you see the all-night
                gas station orbited by gnats
on the edge of the horizon or glowing in the mirror.

NEIGHBORS (IX)

Replace husband with wife. Wife with husband. The kids are always. Seemingly. In our bed. Use knees to raise a tent. A cocoon of floodlit sheets. For metamorphosis. A cave of deep bearing. For hibernation. Later. In their car seats. Your son. Your daughter. Share pretzels. Share goldfish. They call out in intervals. Play the trumpet song. Booker Little. They shout with heads thrown back and beaks open. Play the guitar song. "This Land is Your Land." Reverse roles. Oppose. Stay a molecule. On the other side the sign didn't say nothin'. For you & you & you. The siren sounds. *The thing is* my alter ego said. He wanted this to be a gift. You could tell he wanted to spit. *The thing that triggers a duster is the thing everyone wants—it's about to rain.* Fade to black. Play interlude. Pray the day to open. Be a horse. Be a lion. Be a wolf. Be an elephant. Be a penguin. Siren and swivel a bad skua away. Say a penguin prayer. Rumble. Woman. Rumble. Replace this land with hard land. Open the space between each word. My son says *I'm having an upside down day* and penguins off without pants. His train underwear on inside out. My daughter says *the sky is on my head. Today is my life. The world is in me* and flaps her wings while leaping from the thrift store couch. Mostly. We work opposite hours. Replace hours with shifts. Shifts with light bulbs. So we can see. The light and dark in each other. Look backwards. Replace backwards with upwards. Attune the descent. I love *always*. Let winter in. Replace winter with guests. Exchange guests for little appendages. See the tadpole breath through its skin. Step out of your body. Into blossom. 470 million years ago, arthropods left the sea following plants taking silent root. See the wind scatter. See the robins disperse seeds midflight. 'Leave each scare crow lyin' facedown. / Face down in the dirt.' What cries. What grows here. Where are the fence posts. Leave no stone. Weed not unwanted. We are not afraid. Momentarily. We are where 'the earth sees itself.' Revise you & you & you. Constantly. I love you. An act of imagination you make real through repetition. Stop pulling. 'I know what I am doing.' Be chemical. Be corporeal. Be ethereal. Replace pretense with performance. The earth is bound. Replace bound with blind. Blind with blind trust. Every day I fail. You make promises to the promethean murmurations. Watch the dandelion clock. See the countdown. Replace see with hear. Hear the sudden bird silence. What intercedes in the interstices. Reenact a reenactment. Two minutes to midnight. See the pale tubular stalks and the white drift. The distance, which too will disappear.

Bruce Springsteen

John O'Donohue

Allen Ginsberg

NOTES ON THE WINTER HOLIDAYS

Even you are responsible
            to more than you. My daughter likes visiting
the pet store. *It's like a zoo* she says. She wants
a new calico she can walk with a string. On the way
home she says *do we sing poems before we light candles.*
'Not to see by but to look at.' On one level,
the mind doesn't impose order. The mind
            doesn't impose order. Order presumes
priority. Good credit score. A forwarding address.
My bills accumulate in empty spaces.
My subject position won't stand still.
How did we get here. On one level, we are not
casual acquaintances. Imagine we are pressed
upon one another. For a while we lived
on the second story above The Leader Store
just down the street from The Woolworth's,
which still had a griddle and a soda fountain
and smelled of melted butter. I am not nostalgic.
No need. I can still remember the photographs.
I am a frame. Sometimes a window enclosing
and disclosing. Morning comes on in little bites.
We take the subway to the museum exchanging *yous*
through the tunnel and into the terminal. Imagine
we are pressed against each other. 'Mingled breath
and smell so close.' The silver doors. A cell membrane.
You are a witness only to what you admit. Some words
emit so many possibilities they threaten to burst.
            What is light. What is rain. Now a metaphor.
Take two and answer in the morning. We look
and do more than look. My daughter says
you talk with your eyes off. Why should everything
we see interact with light. I am counting
clouds destined for Florida. I moved the store
here. This is inescapably common. Where
is here. Will you pray with me. Pray with your feet
on the pavement. When she was born we didn't know

Charles Reznikoff

Langston Hughes

68

if she would ever walk. Now she says *my whole body
is a winter storm* as she leaps across the couch upending
the cushions. No digging out. The self is a reintegration
of exponential apologies—a crowd of people
in multi-colored coats, holding handmade signs
and choosing to sit or stand in the same world.
After you. No, I insist. After you.

AND THE FROGS AND TOADS ALL SANG BECAUSE
SINGING WAS EARTHLY

My son and daughter have many aliases. *Stop pretending* argues Frog to Toad. Hop faster. Or you will be eaten. One little leg at a time. Says the addendum at the bottom of the instruction manual in your head on how to build a house out of toothpicks and dixie cups. Why do we need a tiding of magpies. Who calls for a shibboleth. Calls forth. Why do we circle our hands over the cold green ground. Why do we hope to summon a screen of mist. Here we chatter on. Long after. Even inside Badger's belly. We light a candle and set out a picnic. Your end is pending. No, impending. At some point, it seems I've come to believe the seams matter. Frog gives a chocolate chip cookie to Snake who had been laughing criminally all week about animals in swimsuits. Maybe all gifts are down payments on the need for future forgiveness. Toad wears a cerulean dress with tulle, steals marbles from Frog and says, *Blah*. This morning I held Toad over my head and said *You look like a gumdrop*. Toad said *No, you look like a raindrop*, which is infinitely more accurate. I'm infinitely elsewhere. The grindstone is the millstone of progress. Death is simply a shadow that asks *does this make me look fat*. In the meanwhile, Toad throws a handful of legos into the air. See slippage and hegemony in the dictionary. Maybe somewhere around a bend or upon a chestnut tree stump Toad and Frog will meet a gecko named Gramsci who will draw a line in the dust. As for me, I keep thinking about 'bananas ripe and green' in NYC windows. The way we take in the little reflections. The way they reappear to shine out of unexpected places. Like later when Frog says *Grandpa is no longer on our planet*. Like later after all the screeching and transnational trade and canal building, Toad will sit next to Frog while the woods sing and gently place her hand on his hand. It will be as breathing. The fireflies seemingly suspended in the understory. *Look, Frog* said Toad *You are falling from the sky*. The legos hop as they hit the carpet, which is what gravity already narrated for us in the interstices. This is about the moment in the story where the RMS Titanic hits the iceberg but the fiddlers are foxes because of alliteration and Archimedes is an old owl friend who speaks of buoyancy. I'm tired of being an iceberg. Or now by implication in another iteration a plague. Tell us. 'We have heard the music.' The mermaids. Tell us. Let my people go. All people. Then Frog says *Everyone still on this planet is a penguin*. And here. Just before the final turn. For a moment. I believed.

Claude McKay

T.S. Eliot

YOU ARE A CLOCK TOWER IN A DOCUMENTARY FILM THAT MAKES THE SAME SENSE SEEN FROM BEGINNING TO END AND END TO BEGINNING

The ribbon of dirt road to the demolished room of daylight
        and restrained garage in a den of trees
caught from the highway through the ripple of bright grass
suggests a hardening of arteries.

I've come to expect a line of crumbs that disappears into the distance.
I am an internist reader.

The red ants on an assembly line steal
from the ground. Some leave prey
        to the birds. I arrive and never arrive to find you.

I love you. Diminishment. I am interrupted by an internecine
apostrophe. By extension
        you are always beyond the echoed hills. Inexpressible
sonar. Useless and Useful.

I'm tired of being a cricket. Night shifts along the rim of clouds.
Signal. Not yet civil. The bicoastal
        evening swells. Orange contrails deepen and reroute
the sky. Carry their terminus.

The hard part is the earth. But then no one comes running.
It's the boy in the bubble in the background
'and the baby   Paul Simon
with a baboon heart.'

        Looking out. At silence. I speak
as much as I see. Little by little
the feeling of obligation goes where it will do good. Or we hope.
Against the definitive. We are
        almost at the machine barn
braced and tilted on its hilltop.

Even in your sleep   you sing. Little bird
who is allowed to eat.
We come from the sea. I think. Your mother said.
'Not from anything
          we did.' A matter of the break. And now
I come from sea level where time churns
          and 'moves more slowly.' Wave upon wave
                    hurled in front of your feet.
The objectionable content of objects. Unconscionable sense.
Of stumbling upon. Bitter blue sea
glass. So as we shutter or drift toward a mass extinction
some of us gather   as others linger. Lick fingers clean.
As charged.
I wish I could I say
that I could not read. Forward or backward.
          Your performance of self. The beach. The breach.
Hold me.

I am still in my dark carapace
          running my scrapers across my files for you. What I know.
What I withhold.
Will you by angry. When you learn.   Despair. When I cannot know.
Convey. Directly. When.
Or will you simply   not simply   leave what I have left
and think to yourself   and your other selves   *crickets*.

George Oppen

Carlo Rovelli

NEIGHBORS (X)

Replace the light bulb with another light bulb. Borrow a shovel for a burial in the backyard. Keep the shovel ready for a break-in. Repair and repaint the jamb where the crowbar clawed. Replace your home with a structure of wood and glass. Lick the glass shards and walk on coals. What about the stone and mortar foundation. Turn around. Enter before anyone else and check the coastline. Edit the instruction manual in your head. Say a blessing. On some rung of the ladder all prayers abstract. It is embarrassing to live. There are always these imagined conversations that run convergent with our interactions. So *how was your day* is answered with *I think we need more coffee filters* or *'to live means to leave traces. In the interior,* Walter Benjamin *these are accentuated.'* Sometimes we do better with our presence. Or we find our presence where there is need. Or we see how 'the pavement / trembles with light pouring /upon it / Hilda Morley We are held in it' or at least dazzled by 'a puzzling light' buzzing in some category of trees. John Ashbery Other moments we forget leaving the car running in neutral. And when the parking break fails after you've only taken out one child from the back seat and the car slides down the hill and ends up in your front lawn and you panic to see your child and they just look up from the backseat without a thought as to what happened and you revise your own revisions and you break with yourself and you can't stop until you stop and you know that this has to end. We lay with our heads upon each other's chests and listen past the breathing as if the heart was all that murmured. We are neighbors living in the same house. Replace house with hours. Replace hours with ours. Stop redacting in front of me. We are children with children. We 'cannot stand.' We are the murmuration coming to rest and the crisp sky before and after its Abraham Lincoln startling transformation and return.

THE INEFFABLE LIGHT

In the middle of the movie a dinosaur steps upon the neck
of another dinosaur to illustrate the brute binding in our hearts
and a cosmos descends across the screen.
You can view the bones or the cast of bones on display
in the Natural Museum of History.
We are not in competition with nature.
Culture is not other.
Within we persist. At the end
of the day
I photograph the straw-colored light.
The eyes collapse
beneath the tyranny of corn.

The dried cheat grass and nodding foxtail in the roadside gully
        takes the angled light and turns
it into. A kind of longing. A kind of currency.
        It breaks my heart to be this cross-eyed. I go to the bank
to draw water. Please. Return me to me.
Intact. Unincorporated. A field of no-till
        stalks holds a lithe expression of snow.
A minuet of fog and branches resumes.
The starlings peck holes in eggs laid by other birds
        shadow the ground in invasive diamonds
persist so completely
even as the formation
tails off beyond the trail of prairie windbreakers.
Are we perennially blind. Or do we bury what we see.
        What returns. No words on the wind. And yet.
The lay land pond in the deep hollow
waters the Holsteins.
        Some of us upon the decking
beg to be bound. Some of us bind ourselves.

Yesterday on the Great Lakes repairing
        the wooden deck of a raised wreck
concerned only the locals and tourists.
        The ladder disappears. We breathe
a fiction to make other breaths possible. We
have had torrid rain and toured bodies.
        Brushstrokes of people stand.
Imagine the sky open beneath the lip
        of the Ontario. The skin
revealing the repetition of rain. Sometimes
our own water. Sometimes dime-shaped
        moles or the small depression
behind the knee. Round and slowly noted. Once
I sold my labor—extracted—to myself
for a faithless currency.
        Even I could not believe in me.
My fingerprints are not my own
but they are all over
each scene I see.

Of course, there are tears. What do you think
will happen to predictions. Tomorrow
            more rain and more rain
and then none for hundreds of eons. Even if we persist. Whole
            chapters of stars disappear. Cars
saved from mudslides. Forget cars and most other words.
            What words. We have already forgotten
California. Invasive scent of eucalyptus. Now burning pine.
The fires on the hillsides approaching, encroaching
            joining the air with smoke. The nearer the future
the more distant the reply:

It's troubling that words of space and time
        are exchangeable.
If some words are ugly
—and I'm not sure words are since words
are among other things
windows   equations   maps—
        than fungible is ugly.
Are you thinking of mushrooms
        in a redwood forest.
The dark green ferns unfurl. Eat.
Even my heart is replaceable.
        My daughter sings
A heart turned into a person.
A heart turned into a person.
How can a heart turn into a person?
We are closer to the end then we are to the beginning.
We are closing in on Brooklyn again. Imagine the sepia of it all.
        The repetition. The endless endings. Within.
the light. Under the light
        of eternity. I told you
there were dinosaurs in this poem.

Glade glazed in rainwater. The universe.
       we would call human. Call out. White bee.
How much can we lose before. Somewhere
       matter lurches toward consciousness.
A tree in the forest. A forest of concepts.
This is what happens when we talk
       our way into flight.
I think. Love. Come with me. She said.
Lately, I have become obsessed with weather.

THE TRANSDIFFERENTIATION OF ALL THINGS

You said the secret
        is to love our cells
after they become other cells
        in other words
we are dead and we are not dead
        so much atmospheric interference
you fell in love anyway
        with a place that no longer exists
a face that is an afterimage of a face
        lit shallows and then cloud
clarity and sensed erosion
        and you can pick one grain
among many so still a frame
        while in the peaks
flocks of bullnose stingrays
        flash white fins
blur and expose
        green mouths
pero con gracia silenciada

NEIGHBORS (I-X) REVISITED

"the odd branch scrapes across them"
—*Vincent Van Gogh*

Replace one plague with another. And another. Counter plague with prayer and scientific expertise. Redact "please g-d" since the shibboleth is a chrysalis is a crescent moon. On an [insert] field. Moan me. Darling. Mumble. Replace ants with termites. Inside me is another layer of decay. What language do you speak from behind the fence. Could it be a human wall. In encampment. Row upon row of dry tents. Imprisoned in retail space. Exchange grasshoppers for crickets. See how vicious. The volta. You have. The potential to be photographed. I have plaque on my brain. You are not funny. You had me in stitches. In tear gas. Please. Replace my knees since my knees now knock. Even in the oncoming sunshine. Replace with the red light of the exit sign. Exchange sign for music. Dim for din. Too predictable like a whorl of fire. Keep at me. Now the leaves roar via wind. Ob via. Now the crowd overturning the car. Whorls. Now at a distance. Now at an unearned remove. Now walk through the museum. See the docent encroaching. See the missing thorax. The lost abdomen. Specify. See the *Olive Trees*. I carried you 'across the heath and through the hedgerows.' Replace heath with heat.   *Vincent Van Gogh*
See the wall again laden with words. Replace laden with loved. We bear life unevenly. *You have to feed the mule* my alter ego says. Find a river of cars. Which one burns. Does it matter. At which point. Who are we. Come hither. *No matter how good you think the fence is* my alter ego says *the cows will always find a way through*. The rabbit is 'out of hiding.' The dog yelps.   *Robert Frost*
Down the street barking. Replace the wideness of night with quiet. Extract the tincture. We are three letters and a redshift away. Squint hard. See the expanse expanding. Keep at me. We are witnesses to our own evolution. I knew a woman, lovely in her years, who has never bodied pain. What joy if ignorance is. What heartbreak if consciousness is. On a scale. Scale up. A mass. A mask. A scream—pinfire revolver. Herald of mass production. Shootings. Go back. Yonder. Redact evolution. Place tongue against cheek. We are murmuring congregants at a blue wedding. Waiting. Replace wedding with ending. Words inscribed upon doorposts. This time without blood. Do you forget the exodus. The thoughts of the unloved mechanical beetles cross your door. 'The day is green.' Why figure love for warmth. Love can be as cold.   *Wallace Stevens*
The air that makes your breathing visible. Why figure love as sight. I see for some of us. I stop upon the decibel rising. Our relationship is vertical. Inverted. 'I stop somewhere.' And   *Walt Whitman*
we know the daylight makes a museum of the sky. And can be seen through a window. And we volunteer to be volunteered. And we are crickets caught up with song we can no longer hope to display. And O is round. Is final. Is thunder. Is address. Replace moan with mail. So many light seconds ago. O synesthete. 'Last hawser. In you creaks' our 'last longing.' O streets. You   *Pablo Neruda*
are 'filled with rubble. Everything will be different.' Even daylight. 'When we paint.' Our   *Bob Dylan*
symbol. Everywhere. 'You are loosed from your moorings.' Speak what word back. What is   *Frederick Douglass*

the body to us. Microcosm. Abridgement. Hieroglyph. Signature. You are loosed upon the tide and free. We are the embezzled sea speaking in flashes of light. Exchange embezzled for embodied. We are the genderless sea heaving upon the breathless shore. The tired. The poor. The masses. 'Yearning to breathe.' But what we need is (not) also. What we need is. Is. No adherents. And oxygen.

Emma Lazarus

NOTES

The "Neighbors" poems derive their architecture from the poet Sheila McMullin.

"Let There Be Dark" references the four (sometimes five) questions asked at the Passover Seder.

And "there are other earths and skies than these."   Li Po

ACKNOWLEDGEMENTS

Thank you to Amy—my first and last reader—our love is on every page. Thank you to Jack and June whose words are everywhere. Thank you to my mother and father to whom I am deeply indebted for their love and support. A special thanks beyond thanks to John Gallaher, Luke Rolfes, and Richard Sonnemoser for their advice and friendship. Thank you to my colleagues at NWMSU's Department of Language, Literature and Writing for engendering a creative and democratic community. Thank you to Claudia Cortese and Marcela Sulak who reviewed early drafts of this manuscript. Thank you to Tom Renjilian—I could not have asked for a better editor of my work—as well as Tisha Marie Reichle-Aguilera, Laura Roque, & Matt Kessler at Ricochet Editions for taking a chance on this book. Lastly, thank you to the editors of the following journals where these poems, sometimes in different forms and under different titles, first appeared or are forthcoming:

Boiler Journal: Neighbors (II)
Borderlands: Texas Poetry Review: Neighbors (V)
Breakwater Review: Notes on Winter Holidays
Cordite Review: I Gave My Love a Cherry That Had No Stone
Cream City Review: Neighbors (I)
DIAGRAM: But For the Grace
FIELD: We Move in Abundance & We Live in an Unknown Sea
Fourteen Hills: It's Difficult to Stop Thinking About a Cadillac Orbiting the Earth
Hayden's Ferry Review: The New Light
Inflectionist Review: a) When the Clouds Break Suggests a Sudden Upheaval in the Heart & c) When the Clouds Break We Take in a Kind of Daily Repetition
Jellyfish Magazine: Archaeology of Air
Map Literary: Neighbors (VI), Neighbors (VII) & Neighbors (I-X) Revisited
Mid-American Review: Let There Be Dark
minnesota review: The Sea as Far as We Know
New Orleans Review: Henny Penny Blues & The Light Walks Other Avenues
nonsite.org: Every Meeting is a Hallucination Waiting to Happen
Painted Bride Quarterly: Neighbors (III) & Neighbors (IV)
RHINO Poetry: The Absurdity of Carrying an Umbrella When All You Need Is Oiled Feathers
Salt Hill Journal: Neighbors (X)

DANIEL BIEGELSON is the author of the book *of being neighbors* (Ricochet Editions) and the chapbook *Only the Borrowed Light* (VERSE). He serves as the Director of the Visiting Writers Series at Northwest Missouri State University, where he also works as an editor for *The Laurel Review*. He holds an MFA from the University of Montana, an MA from the University of Massachusetts—Amherst, hails from New Jersey and lives near Kansas City with his wife and children.